All you need to know about Montenegro

Copyright © 2024 Jonas Hoffmann-Schmidt.
Translation: Linda Amber Chambers.

All rights reserved. This book, including all its parts, is protected by copyright. Any use outside the narrow limits of copyright law is prohibited without the written consent of the author. This book has been created using artificial intelligence to provide unique and informative content.

Disclaimer: This book is for entertainment purposes only. The information, facts and views contained therein have been researched and compiled to the best of our knowledge and belief. Nevertheless, the author and the publisher assume no liability for the accuracy or completeness of the information. Readers should consult with professionals before making any decisions based on this information. Use of this book is the responsibility of the reader.

Introduction 6

The geography of Montenegro 8

Montenegro's climate and weather 10

The History of Montenegro: From the Beginnings to Independence 12

The era of the Principality of Montenegro 15

Montenegro in the First World War 17

The Emergence of Modern Montenegro 19

Montenegro's political development 21

The economy of Montenegro 24

The people and culture of Montenegro 27

Montenegro's language and dialects 30

Die Religion in Montenegro 32

Montenegro's National Holidays and Customs 34

The Art Scene of Montenegro 36

Montenegro's traditional music and dances 38

Montenegro's culinary diversity 40

Montenegrin specialties and dishes 42

Wine culture in Montenegro 45

Montenegro's wildlife and natural treasures 47

National parks and nature reserves in Montenegro 50

The Adriatic coast of Montenegro 53

The beaches and bays of Montenegro 56

The Bay of Kotor and its history 59

Budva: history and sights 62

The Old Town of Kotor and its Significance 64

Cetinje: The historic capital of Montenegro 67

Podgorica: Moderne Metropole im Landesinneren 69

Bar: Historic harbour and cultural city 72

Herceg Novi: Pearl of the Bay of Kotor 74

Ulcinj: The southernmost city of Montenegro 76

The Eastern Cape of Montenegro 78

The historical significance of Eastern Montenegro 80

The Orthodox monasteries of Montenegro 82

Montenegro's fortifications and castles 84

The UNESCO World Heritage Sites in Montenegro 86

Top Montenegro's Water Sports Facilities 88

Hiking and outdoor activities in Montenegro 90

Montenegro's traditional craftsmanship 92

The Montenegrins and their hospitality 94

Travel and accommodation in Montenegro 96

Transportation and Transportation in Montenegro 98

Practical information for travellers 101

Safety and health in Montenegro 104

Montenegro: Looking to the future 107

Closing remarks 110

Introduction

Montenegro, a small country on the Adriatic coast in southeastern Europe, has become an increasingly popular tourist destination in recent decades. This part of the world holds an abundance of natural beauty, cultural diversity, and historical significance to explore.

With an area of around 13,812 square kilometers, Montenegro is one of the smallest countries in Europe. Nevertheless, it is a country of great diversity and impressive scenic beauty. The coastline stretches for about 293 kilometers along the Adriatic Sea, offering breathtaking views of the sparkling sea, picturesque bays, and charming coastal towns.

The interior of Montenegro, on the other hand, is dominated by majestic mountains. The Dinaric Mountains span much of the country and provide a dramatic backdrop for outdoor adventures, including hiking, mountaineering, and whitewater rafting. The highest peak, Bobotov Kuk, rises a proud 2,522 meters into the air.

Montenegro's history goes back a long way, and the country has experienced an eventful past. The first settlements in this region date back to ancient times, and Montenegro was once a major player in the conflicts and alliances of the

Balkans. Over the centuries, the country has witnessed the rule of various empires and empires, including the Romans, Byzantines, Venetians, and Ottomans.

Montenegro's development into an independent state came relatively late, and it was not until 2006 that it declared its independence from the former Federal Republic of Yugoslavia. Since then, the country has retained its sovereignty and is a member of various international organizations, including the United Nations and NATO.

Montenegro's population is diverse and consists of various ethnic groups, including Montenegrins, Serbs, Bosniaks, Albanians, and many more. The official language is Montenegrin, but many people also speak Serbian, Bosnian, Albanian, and other languages.

In the upcoming chapters, we will take an in-depth look at the various aspects of this fascinating country, starting from its rich history to its stunning nature and its unique culture and way of life. Montenegro offers a remarkable diversity to discover, and we will embark on this journey of discovery together in the following pages.

The geography of Montenegro

Montenegro, a small country in southeastern Europe, impresses with its diverse and impressive geography. It covers an area of about 13,812 square kilometers and is located in the Balkans, bordering Serbia to the north and east, Albania to the south, Croatia to the west and the Adriatic Sea to the southwest.

Montenegro's coastline stretches for about 293 kilometers along the Adriatic coast and offers a spectacular mix of picturesque bays, dreamy beaches and charming coastal towns. The Bay of Kotor, also known as "Europe's southernmost fjord", is a prominent geographical feature. This bay, cut deep into the land, stretches for 28 kilometers and is surrounded by high mountain ranges. The old town of Kotor, a UNESCO World Heritage Site, is located on the shore of this bay and is of historical importance.

In the interior of Montenegro, the Dinaric Mountains dominate the landscape. These majestic mountain ranges not only offer a breathtaking backdrop, but also numerous opportunities for outdoor enthusiasts. Montenegro's highest peak, Bobotov Kuk, rises an impressive 2,522 meters and offers spectacular views of the surrounding region.

The country is rich in rivers and lakes, including Lake Skadar, the largest lake in the Balkans. This lake covers an area of around 370 square kilometres and is home to a rich variety of animal and plant species. The Tara River, known for its spectacular Tara Gorge, is also a notable geographical feature of Montenegro.

The coastal plain and the interior have different climatic conditions. While the coast enjoys a Mediterranean climate with mild winters and warm summers, the mountainous region is characterized by a continental climate, which leads to strong temperature fluctuations between seasons.

Montenegro's geographical diversity, from the coast to the mountains and rivers, makes it a unique and fascinating destination. In the following chapters, we will take a closer look at the different aspects of this geographical diversity and its impact on the land, culture and way of life of the people.

Montenegro's climate and weather

The climate in Montenegro is characterized by its geographical location on the Adriatic coast and the influences of the Dinaric Mountains inland. The country has a variety of climatic conditions that differ depending on the region and altitude.

The Adriatic coast has a Mediterranean climate. Summers here are hot and dry, with average temperatures often exceeding 30 degrees Celsius in July and August. Winters are mild and humid, with temperatures rarely below freezing. The amount of precipitation on the coast is comparatively low and is mainly concentrated in the winter months.

In the interior, especially in the mountainous regions, a continental climate prevails. Here, summers tend to be milder and winters colder than on the coast. Temperatures can drop below freezing in winter, especially in the higher elevations of the Dinaric Mountains. Snow is often found in the mountain regions in winter and offers opportunities for winter sports activities.

The Tara Gorge, one of the deepest gorges in the world and part of the Dinaric Mountains, significantly influences the local microclimate. Temperatures in the gorge can be very high in summer, while there are often sharp drops in temperature in winter.

Another important climatic feature in Montenegro is the Bora wind, a cold fall wind that blows from the northeast. This wind can reach extreme wind speeds, especially on the Adriatic coast, and have a significant impact on weather patterns.

Montenegro offers various opportunities for outdoor activities due to its climatic diversity. While the coast offers ideal conditions for beach holidays in summer, the mountains attract winter sports enthusiasts in winter. The Mediterranean climate and abundant sunlight have also made Montenegro an up-and-coming destination for viticulture.

The different climatic conditions in Montenegro are reflected in the flora and fauna of the country, influencing agriculture, the way of life of the people and cultural traditions. In the following chapters, we will go into more detail about these aspects and further explore the effects of climate and weather on Montenegro.

The History of Montenegro: From the Beginnings to Independence

The history of Montenegro is rich in events and shaped by a variety of influences from the region and beyond. Its origins date back a long way, to the time of the ancient settlements and tribes that inhabited this region.

The first records of the area that is now Montenegro date back to ancient times. In the Roman era, this region was part of the province of Dalmatia and was settled and ruled by the Romans. After the fall of the Roman Empire in the 5th century, parts of present-day Montenegro were settled by various peoples, including Slavs, Avars and Byzantines.

In the Middle Ages, several independent principalities and duchies developed on the territory of Montenegro. These small empires were often involved in conflicts with neighboring powers such as the Byzantine Empire, Venice, and the Ottoman Empire. During this time, the concept of a Montenegrin people and its own identity based on Orthodox Christianity emerged.

The Ottoman conquest began in the 15th century and led to the long-lasting rule of the Ottoman Empire over parts of Montenegro. During this time, the Montenegrin clans became important actors in the resistance against the Ottomans. This period of Ottoman rule lasted until the late 17th century, when the Petrović-Njegoš clan took over and founded the Principality of Montenegro.

In the 19th century, Montenegro experienced a period of expansion and territorial gains against the Ottomans. Prince-Bishop Petar II Petrović-Njegoš played a decisive role in this development. In 1878, Montenegro was internationally recognized at the Congress of Berlin and received additional territories.

During the First World War, Montenegro fought on the side of the Allies, but was occupied by the Austro-Hungarian troops. After the war, it merged with Serbia to form a common kingdom, which later became part of the Kingdom of Yugoslavia.

The period of socialist Yugoslavia brought political and economic changes to Montenegro. After the collapse of Yugoslavia, Montenegro declared its independence from the Federal Republic of

Yugoslavia in 1992 and finally became an independent state in 2006 after a referendum.

This historic journey from the beginnings of Montenegro to independence in the 21st century reflects the complex and chequered history of this fascinating country. In the coming chapters, we will explore more details about the different eras and developments in Montenegro in order to draw a comprehensive picture of its history.

The era of the Principality of Montenegro

The era of the Principality of Montenegro, also known as the time of the Prince-Bishop, was a crucial period in the history of Montenegro that transformed the country into an independent and sovereign entity.

The roots of the Principality of Montenegro date back to the 15th century, when the country was under Ottoman rule. The Montenegrins, under the leadership of local princes and clans, began to rise up against Ottoman domination. This resistance led to the area in the interior of Montenegro serving as a refuge for those who wanted to escape Ottoman control.

In the 17th century, the Petrović-Njegoš clan, led by Danilo Petrović-Njegoš, came to the fore as a decisive player. Danilo was elected Prince-Bishop of Montenegro in 1696 and began a policy of strengthening Montenegrin independence. He introduced reforms and promoted education and culture in the country.

During his reign, Danilo Petrović-Njegoš sought the recognition of Montenegro as an independent principality. This was achieved in 1852 with recognition by the Ottoman Empire. Danilo became the first prince of Montenegro and led the country into the principality phase.

The era of the Principality of Montenegro was marked by constant conflicts with the Ottomans. The Montenegrins vigorously defended their independence and their territories. A climax of this conflict was the Montenegrin-Ottoman War of 1876-1878, which led to the territorial expansion of Montenegro.

The princely status of Montenegro was officially recognized in 1910, and the Principality of Montenegro was created with Nikola I Petrović-Njegoš as prince. During his reign, Montenegro underwent modernization and expanded its diplomatic relations with other European nations.

The era of the Principality of Montenegro was an important step on the way to the country's independence and sovereignty. It marked the transition from an area under Ottoman rule to an independent state. The events and developments during this period shaped the identity and political culture of Montenegro and laid the foundation for the country's later history.

Montenegro in the First World War

The First World War, which raged from 1914 to 1918, also had a significant impact on Montenegro, which was an independent principality at the time. The war years brought profound changes and challenges for the country and its people.

Montenegro joined the First World War on the side of the Entente powers, which also included Great Britain, France and Russia. The decision to enter the war was shaped by political and strategic considerations. Prince Nikola I Petrović-Njegoš hoped for territorial gains and the support of the Entente for the independence and preservation of Montenegro as an independent state.

The war began for Montenegro on August 8, 1914, when it declared war on Austria-Hungary. This led to an invasion of Austro-Hungarian troops into the country. Montenegro and its allies initially fought successfully against the Austro-Hungarian army and made some territorial gains.

However, the tide changed in the course of the war. Montenegro was put under considerable pressure by the Central Powers, including the German Reich and Austria-Hungary. Supply lines were cut off, leading to a serious deterioration in the country's economic and military situation.

The situation deteriorated further when the invasion of Central Power troops began in January 1916. Montenegro was unable to withstand the attacks and was forced to retreat. The capital Cetinje was captured by the Austro-Hungarian troops, and the government fled into exile.

During the retreat and fighting in the mountains, Montenegro suffered heavy losses, both military and civilian. The war had a devastating impact on the country's economy, infrastructure and population.

After the end of the First World War and the collapse of the Central Powers, Montenegro regained its independence. The country joined the newly formed Kingdom of Serbs, Croats and Slovenes, which was later renamed Yugoslavia.

Montenegro's participation in the First World War was short-lived, but it left deep traces in the country's history. The war years were marked by suffering and losses and had a long-term impact on Montenegro's political development in the interwar period and beyond.

The Emergence of Modern Montenegro

The emergence of modern Montenegro is a fascinating chapter in the history of this small Balkan country. It is closely linked to the political changes and geopolitical upheavals of the 20th century.

After the end of World War I and the collapse of the Central Powers, Montenegro joined the Kingdom of Serbs, Croats and Slovenes in 1918, which later became known as Yugoslavia. This political alliance marked a crucial turning point in Montenegro's history, as it limited the country's autonomy and placed it within the framework of the Yugoslav state.

In the decades that followed, Montenegro tried to preserve its identity and cultural independence within Yugoslavia. The Montenegrin language and culture have been actively promoted, and the history of the Principality of Montenegro has been revived to strengthen national awareness.

During World War II, Yugoslavia was occupied by German and Italian troops, and Montenegro was split in two. One part of the country came under Italian control, while the other was occupied by the German Wehrmacht. During the war, there was also a communist partisan movement led by Josip Broz Tito, who later became the first president of Yugoslavia.

After the end of World War II and the victory of the partisans, Yugoslavia was transformed into a socialist federal republic. Montenegro was one of the six constituent republics of Yugoslavia and retained a certain autonomy within the federal system.

However, the relationship between Montenegro and the Yugoslav central state has often been marked by tensions and conflicts. In the 1980s, nationalist currents in Yugoslavia increased, and this ultimately led to the country's disintegration in the 1990s.

On 3 June 2006, Montenegro declared its independence from Serbia following a referendum overseen by the European Union. This marked the birth of modern Montenegro as an independent state.

The emergence of modern Montenegro was a complex process, marked by political changes, social movements and geopolitical developments. Today, Montenegro is a sovereign state and a member of international organizations such as the United Nations and NATO, while preserving its own identity and culture.

Montenegro's political development

The political development of Montenegro is a complex and multi-layered topic that runs through the country's history from its beginnings to the present day. This development reflects the different political ideologies, power struggles and geopolitical influences that have shaped the country.

During the Middle Ages, Montenegro consisted of various principalities and duchies, often operating independently of each other. The political structure was characterized by local clans and leaders who enjoyed some autonomy in their respective territories. However, the country was also subject to the influence of neighboring powers such as the Byzantine Empire, Venice, and the Ottoman Empire.

In the 19th century, Montenegro began a period of modernization and political restructuring under the leadership of Prince Danilo Petrović-Njegoš. The country's independence was internationally recognized at the Congress of Berlin in 1878, and Montenegro became a principality with Danilo as the first prince.

The political landscape changed again in 1910, when Prince Nikola I Petrović-Njegoš proclaimed the monarchy and declared himself king. Montenegro remained an independent kingdom until the end of World War I, when it joined the newly formed Kingdom of Serbs, Croats, and Slovenes.

During the period of socialist Yugoslavia after World War II, Montenegro retained its political integration within the framework of federal Yugoslavia. The communist party Japanska Komunistička Partija (JKP) dominated the political scene and led the country through the socialist era.

In the 1990s, when Yugoslavia broke up, Montenegro experienced political turmoil and uncertainty. The independence movement gained momentum, and in 2006 Montenegro finally declared its independence from Serbia after a referendum.

Since its independence, Montenegro has undergone a political development characterized by efforts towards democratization, European integration and economic reforms. The country has been actively seeking membership in international organizations such as NATO and the European Union.

Montenegro's political development reflects the challenges and opportunities that this small Balkan country has overcome throughout its history. Montenegro's political future will continue to be shaped by the dynamic forces of international politics and the needs of its citizens.

The economy of Montenegro

Montenegro's economy has undergone a remarkable transformation over the years. This small Balkan country, which was established as an independent state after its independence in 2006, has evolved from a socialist economy to a market-economy orientation.

During the period of socialist Yugoslavia, to which Montenegro belonged, the economy was highly centralized and dominated by state-owned enterprises. However, this changed in the 1990s when Yugoslavia fell apart and Montenegro sought independence. The country began to introduce economic reforms in order to break away from the socialist planned economy.

An important step in this development was the introduction of the German mark (later euro) as the official currency of Montenegro in 2002. This created stability and confidence in the country's economy and facilitated trade with European partners.

Montenegro also pursued a policy of economic liberalization and privatization of state-owned enterprises. This led to the emergence of a sector of small and medium-sized enterprises and the promotion of foreign investment. The tourism sector developed into an important source of income as Montenegro promoted its natural beauty and coastline.

Montenegro's geographical location on the Adriatic coast has made it an attractive destination for tourists from all over the world. The numerous beaches, picturesque bays and historic towns attract thousands of visitors every year. The tourism sector has contributed significantly to the country's economic growth in recent years.

Montenegro has also invested in renewable energy and modernized its energy infrastructure. This has helped reduce dependence on fossil fuels and increase energy efficiency.

Despite this progress, Montenegro still faces economic challenges. Unemployment remains a problem and income inequality is palpable. In addition, structural reforms are needed in areas such as education, health care and public administration.

Montenegro continues to strive for its integration into the European Union and NATO, which brings potential economic benefits. The country's economic future will depend on its ability to drive economic diversification, improve infrastructure, and maintain economic stability.

Montenegro's economy reflects the challenges and opportunities of a young state that is on the path to economic growth and development. The next few years will be crucial to realize the country's goals and ambitions.

The people and culture of Montenegro

The people and culture of Montenegro are as diverse and fascinating as the country's geographical landscape. Montenegro is a melting pot of different ethnic groups and cultural influences, which has resulted in a rich and multifaceted culture.

The Montenegrin population consists mainly of Montenegrins, Serbs, Bosnians, Albanians and Croats. This diversity reflects the historical development of the region and has contributed to the emergence of a multicultural society.

The Montenegrin language, a South Slavic language, is spoken by the majority of the population. It is closely related to the Serbian, Croatian and Bosnian languages and has its own regional dialects. Montenegrin culture and identity are strongly linked to language and are expressed through literary works, music and folklore.

Religion also plays an important role in Montenegro, with the majority of the population belonging to Orthodox Christianity. There is also a significant Muslim minority, mainly in the Sandžak region in the east of the country, as well as a Catholic minority in some coastal areas.

The traditional Montenegrin culture is rich in folklore, music and dance. Traditional Montenegrin music, known as "Starogradska muzika", is characterized by the sounds of the mandolin, flute and tambourine. Montenegrin dances, such as the "Oro", are widely used at festivals and celebrations and reflect the joie de vivre and pride of the people.

Montenegrin cuisine is influenced by the country's geographical location and is characterized by Mediterranean and Balkan influences. Fresh fish, olive oil, cheese, meat dishes and vegetables are widely used in traditional cuisine. Montenegro is also known for its wine, especially in the region around Lake Skadar.

Montenegrin culture is closely linked to nature, as the country offers stunning natural beauty. The Montenegrin people appreciate the mountains, rivers, lakes and the Adriatic coast, and nature plays an important role in their life and culture.

In recent years, Montenegro has increasingly invested in cultural events and festivals to promote and preserve the country's cultural diversity. The country also has a thriving art scene, which is reflected in galleries, theaters, and music venues.

The people and culture of Montenegro are shaped by a rich history, cultural traditions and the beauty of the natural environment. This makes Montenegro a unique and fascinating place worth discovering and exploring.

Montenegro's language and dialects

The language in Montenegro is a multi-layered and multifaceted subject that reflects the country's rich cultural and historical diversity. The official language of Montenegro is Montenegrin, which belongs to the group of South Slavic languages and is closely related to Serbian, Croatian and Bosnian.

Montenegrin is spoken as a native language by the majority of the population, and there are regional dialects and accents that can be found in different parts of the country. These dialects are often influenced by historical and geographical factors.

Some of the most significant dialects in Montenegro are the Zeta dialect, which is spoken in the Zeta region and the capital Podgorica, as well as the Bavarian dialect, which is used in the Bay of Kotor and the surrounding areas. These dialects have differences in pronunciation, grammar and vocabulary that set them apart from other South Slavic languages.

The question of language in Montenegro has historically been the subject of political and cultural debate. During the period of socialist Yugoslavia, the language was often referred to as Serbo-Croatian to emphasize the cultural unity within the federal state. After Montenegro's independence in 2006, Montenegrin was recognized as a language in its own right and was given its own standard.

The Montenegrin language uses the Latin alphabet, similar to Croatian and Bosnian, but there is also a Cyrillic version. Both alphabets are officially recognized and are used in education and public documents.

The language in Montenegro reflects the diversity and cultural influences of the country. Despite the different dialects and historical debates, the Montenegrin language has played an important role in the country's identity and culture, contributing to the diversity and unity of Montenegro.

Die Religion in Montenegro

Religion in Montenegro reflects the diversity of the population and its historical development. The country is shaped by a wide range of religious beliefs and practices that have evolved over the centuries.

The majority of the Montenegrin population belongs to the Orthodox Christian Church, more precisely the Serbian Orthodox Church. This Orthodox tradition has deep roots in Montenegro and is an important part of the identity of many people in the country. The Serbian Orthodox Church has a long history in Montenegro and plays a central role in religious and cultural life.

Another important religious group in Montenegro are the Muslims, mainly from the Bosniak population in the Sandžak region. Islam has a long history in this region and is an important part of the religious landscape. The majority of Montenegrin Muslims belong to the Sunni tradition.

There is also a Catholic minority in Montenegro, mainly in the coastal areas. The Catholic Church has historical roots in Montenegro and is particularly present in cities such as Kotor and Herceg Novi. The

Roman Catholic tradition is maintained by the Croatian and Albanian population.

In addition to these main religions, there are also smaller religious communities and beliefs in Montenegro, including various Protestant denominations and other religious minorities.

Freedom of religion is constitutionally guaranteed in Montenegro, and the government protects the rights of religious communities. The country's religious diversity is reflected in its numerous religious buildings and sites, including churches, mosques, and monasteries.

Religion plays an important role in the daily life of the people of Montenegro and influences aspects such as culture, customs and celebrations. Religious festivals and rituals are deeply rooted in society and contribute to identity and social cohesion.

Religion in Montenegro is a diverse and dynamic element of society that shapes the country's history and cultural landscape. Despite the differences in faith and practice, there is a sense of tolerance and cohesion among the different religious communities that enriches the diversity of the country.

Montenegro's National Holidays and Customs

Montenegro celebrates a variety of national holidays and customs that are deeply rooted in its history, culture, and tradition. These holidays and customs reflect the identity and values of the country and are of great importance to the Montenegrin people.

An important national holiday in Montenegro is Independence Day, which is celebrated on May 21. This day marks Montenegro's declaration of independence in 2006, after the country left the State Union of Serbia and Montenegro. The celebrations on this day include parades, concerts and cultural events that highlight the national consciousness and sovereignty of Montenegro.

Another important holiday is the National Day, which is celebrated on July 13. This day commemorates the Battle of Kosovo Polje in 1389, which has significant historical significance for Serbian and Montenegrin history. People often gather in churches and monasteries to attend services and honor the victims of the battle.

Orthodox holidays play a central role in Montenegro's religious calendar. Christmas,

Easter and other religious festivals are celebrated with church services, processions and celebrations. These holidays are marked by religious devotion and traditions that have been passed down for generations.

Montenegro is also home to numerous regional customs and festivals that are shaped by local culture and history. For example, the coastal region celebrates "Boka Night", a festival that honors the region's rich maritime tradition. In the mountainous regions, there are traditional festivals that focus on agriculture and rural life.

Montenegrin culture is rich in music and dance, and many customs are closely linked to musical performances. Folk music and dances such as the "Oro" are an integral part of the celebrations at weddings, festivals and other occasions.

The people of Montenegro are proud of their traditions and customs and preserve them with great care. These holidays and customs are an important source of identity and cohesion in Montenegrin society and contribute to the preservation of the country's cultural diversity.

The Art Scene of Montenegro

Montenegro's art scene is characterized by a rich cultural history and a growing contemporary scene. This small Balkan country has a diverse and vibrant art world that reflects the cultural identity and creativity of the Montenegrin population.

The roots of Montenegrin art go far back in history. In the medieval period, Montenegrin artists created religious works of art, including icons and frescoes, which can be found in monasteries and churches throughout the country. These works of art bear witness to a deep religious connection and a rich cultural heritage.

In the 19th century, Montenegro experienced a cultural heyday, marked by Prince Danilo Petrović-Njegoš and his interest in education and culture. Montenegrin poets, writers and painters such as Petar II Petrović-Njegoš contributed to the development of their own cultural identity.

Montenegro's modern art scene has evolved since its independence in 2006. The country has a growing number of galleries, museums, and art schools that promote and showcase the creativity of artists. The capital Podgorica and the coastal city of Kotor are centers for the contemporary art scene.

Montenegrin artists work in various mediums, including painting, sculpture, photography, performance, and installation. The themes of her art are often inspired by the nature, history, society and identity of the country.

Music also plays an important role in Montenegro's art scene. Traditional Montenegrin music, known as "Starogradska muzika", is often played at festivals and celebrations. There is also a growing modern music scene that includes rock, pop, and electronic music.

Montenegrin literature has a long tradition that dates back to the Middle Ages. Numerous Montenegrin writers have created significant works in the fields of prose, poetry and drama and contribute to the country's literary diversity.

Montenegro's art scene reflects the diversity and creativity of Montenegrin culture. Artists from the country are recognized nationally and internationally, helping to preserve and develop Montenegro's cultural diversity and artistic heritage. The art scene is an important part of the country's identity and contributes to the enrichment of the cultural landscape.

Montenegro's traditional music and dances

The traditional music and dances of Montenegro are a living expression of the country's rich cultural traditions and heritage. These forms of folk art are deeply embedded in the history and daily life of the Montenegrin population and reflect the country's identity and values.

Traditional Montenegrin music is diverse and varies from region to region. One of the most famous musical traditions is the "Starogradska muzika" or "Old Town Music". This musical genre originated in the cities of Montenegro and is characterized by melodies played on traditional instruments such as the mandolin, flute and tambourine. The lyrics of the songs often tell of love, home and life in the cities.

Another important musical element in Montenegro is the "gusle". This is a traditional instrument that resembles a one-piece string instrument and is often accompanied by a singer. The "gusle" is often used in epic songs and stories that honor the history and heroes of Montenegro.

The traditional dances of Montenegro are as diverse as the music. One of the most famous dances is the "Oro", a circle dance that is widely used at festivals and celebrations. This dance symbolizes the community and cohesion of the people of Montenegro and is often accompanied by traditional music.

Another traditional dance is the "Kolo", a group dance in which the dancers dance in a circle and hold hands. This dance is a symbol of the solidarity of the Montenegrin community and is often performed at weddings and celebrations.

The traditional music and dances of Montenegro are an important part of the country's cultural heritage. They reflect the history, values and joie de vivre of the Montenegrin people and are celebrated in various occasions and festivals throughout Montenegro. These forms of folk art are alive and important for the country's cultural identity.

Montenegro's culinary diversity

Montenegro's culinary diversity reflects the country's rich history and geographical location. This diversity extends from the coastal regions along the Adriatic coast to the mountainous areas inland, offering the insight into a culinary journey marked by different influences and traditions.

Montenegrin cuisine is influenced by Mediterranean and Balkan influences, with fresh ingredients such as fish, olive oil, vegetables, cheese and meat playing a central role. Some of Montenegro's most famous dishes are "Pasticada", a braised meat dish, "Buzara", a seafood pasta, and "Kacamak", a dish made of corn porridge and cheese.

The coastal region of Montenegro offers a rich selection of seafood, including fish, mussels and octopus. The fresh ingredients are often prepared with herbs, garlic and olive oil and ensure aromatic and tasty cuisine.

In the mountainous areas of the country, the cuisine is dominated by rustic dishes that reflect the needs of farmers and shepherds. Meat dishes such as lamb, pork and beef are popular and are often grilled or stewed.

"Kajmak", a type of cream cheese, is a common accompaniment to many dishes.

Another culinary speciality in Montenegro is viticulture. The country has a long tradition of wine production, and the vineyards stretch along the coast and inland. Montenegrin wine is usually of high quality and is produced in many different varieties.

The pastry shop in Montenegro is also rich, with a variety of desserts and sweets. "Palačinke", thin pancakes filled with jam or chocolate, are a popular dessert, as is "rozata", a creamy dessert with caramel sauce.

Montenegro's culinary diversity reflects the diversity of the regions and the cultural influences that the country has experienced over the centuries. Montenegrin cuisine is a delight for the senses and offers a rich selection of taste experiences that reflect the cultural identity and hospitality of the country. It is worth discovering and enjoying the different culinary traditions of Montenegro.

Montenegrin specialties and dishes

Montenegrin cuisine is characterized by a rich variety of specialties and dishes that reflect the culinary creativity and rich history of the country. From the coastal areas along the Adriatic coast to the mountainous regions inland, Montenegro offers a wealth of taste experiences that delight the senses.

One of the most famous Montenegrin specialties is "Njeguški pršut". This is air-dried ham produced in the Njeguši region, near Kotor. The ham is salted and air-dried in the traditional way, which gives it its unique flavor and texture. It is often thinly sliced and served as an appetizer or snack.

Another famous Montenegrin dish is "Ćevapi". These grilled minced meat rolls are usually made from mixed beef and lamb and served with onions, ajvar (a paprika paste), and bread. Ćevapi are a popular street food dish and are often served at barbecues and restaurants.

"Riblja čorba" is a hearty fish soup that is very popular in Montenegro. It is prepared from various types of fish, vegetables, peppers and spices and has an intense taste. This soup is a must for fish lovers and is often served as a main course.

In the coastal areas, seafood such as mussels, squid and octopus are common. These are often grilled, fried or prepared in various sauces. "Paštrovski makaruli" is a local pasta speciality from the Paštrovačka region, served with cheese and cream.

Montenegro's mountainous regions are known for hearty dishes, including "Karađorđeva šnicla", a schnitzel filled with cheese and ham, and "Kuvana govedina", a braised beef dish. These dishes are perfect for the cold winter months and are often enjoyed by the locals.

The variety of Montenegrin cuisine also extends to desserts. "Palačinke" are thin pancakes that are often filled with jam, chocolate or nuts. "Krofne" are donuts dusted with powdered sugar that are a sweet temptation.

Montenegro is also proud of its wine tradition. The vineyards along the coast and inland produce a wide range of wines, including red, white and rosé wines. Montenegrin wine is known for its quality and is often counted among the country's specialties.

Montenegrin cuisine is rich in aromas and taste sensations that are shaped by the diversity of the regions and the rich cultural history of the country. The specialties and dishes of Montenegro are an important part of the country's cultural identity and offer visitors a unique opportunity to discover and enjoy the culinary diversity.

Wine culture in Montenegro

Wine culture in Montenegro has a long and rich history that dates back to ancient times. The country has a variety of wine-growing areas that stretch along the coastal regions and inland. Montenegrin wine culture is closely linked to the country's identity and traditions and has evolved over the centuries.

One of the most famous wine regions in Montenegro is the Bay of Kotor, which is known for its picturesque vineyards and mild Mediterranean climate. Mainly red varieties such as Vranac and Kratošija are grown here. Vranac is the most famous grape in Montenegro and produces a powerful red wine with fruity aromas and a deep color. This grape is a symbol of Montenegrin wine culture and is often grown in the vineyards of the region.

Inland, especially in the mountainous regions, a variety of grape varieties are grown, including Cabernet Sauvignon, Merlot, and Chardonnay. These regions benefit from cooler temperatures and offer ideal conditions for growing white wine grapes.

Montenegrin winemaking follows traditional methods that have been passed down for generations. The grapes are harvested by hand and carefully processed in wine cellars. Storage is often done in wooden barrels to refine the wine and give it complex aromas.

Montenegrin wine is appreciated both nationally and internationally and has received numerous awards and recognitions. Wine culture is an important part of the country's culinary heritage and is celebrated in many festive occasions and celebrations.

In Montenegro, wine is not only a luxury food, but also a symbol of hospitality and community. Wine tasting is a popular activity for tourists, who have the opportunity to discover the diversity of Montenegrin wines and experience the country's hospitable culture.

Wine culture in Montenegro is an important part of the country's cultural identity and a symbol of its rich history and traditions. The variety of grape varieties, the quality of the wines and the passion of the winemakers contribute to establishing Montenegro as an emerging wine country in the region.

Montenegro's wildlife and natural treasures

Montenegro is home to an impressive variety of animal species and natural treasures that reflect the unspoiled beauty and diversity of nature in this Balkan country. The unique geographical location between the Adriatic coast and the majestic mountains creates a diverse ecosystem that is home to numerous animal species.

The coastal region of Montenegro is known for its picturesque beaches and the clear waters of the Adriatic Sea. Various sea creatures can be found here, including dolphins, tuna, turtles, and a variety of fish species. The Adriatic coast is an important habitat for these marine species, attracting divers and nature lovers from all over the world.

Montenegro's mountains, such as Durmitor National Park, Biogradska Gora National Park, and Prokletije Mountains, are home to abundant wildlife. Brown bears, wolves, lynxes, wild boars and deer are just some of the mammals that call these pristine forests and mountains home. The European brown bear is particularly noteworthy, as

Montenegro is one of the last refuges for this endangered species in Europe.

Birdwatchers will be amazed by the variety of bird species in Montenegro. The pristine lakes and wetlands provide habitat for waterfowl such as cranes, pelicans, herons, and ducks. These areas are important breeding grounds for many species and contribute to the preservation of biodiversity.

Montenegro's rivers and lakes are rich in fish species, including trout, grayling and perch. Fishing is a popular activity for locals and tourists alike, and the clear waters provide ideal conditions for this sport.

Montenegro is also proud of its endemic species, which are found only in this country. These include the Montenegro pine, a rare tree that grows in the mountainous regions, as well as the Ohrid mud snail, a unique species of water snail that lives in Lake Ohrid.

The natural treasures of Montenegro are not only a source of beauty, but also of great ecological importance. The country is actively involved in nature conservation and has established many protected areas to preserve wildlife and natural habitats.

Montenegro's wildlife and natural treasures are an important part of the country's identity and heritage. They offer visitors the opportunity to experience the untouched beauty of nature and contribute to the preservation of biodiversity in the region. Montenegro is a true paradise for nature lovers and adventurers who want to explore the country's wildlife and natural treasures.

National parks and nature reserves in Montenegro

Montenegro prides itself on its rich natural diversity and has created an impressive number of national parks and nature reserves to protect and preserve these treasures. These protected areas span the entire country and offer stunning scenery, abundant wildlife, and a unique opportunity to experience Montenegro's unspoiled nature.

One of the most famous national parks in Montenegro is Durmitor National Park, which is also a UNESCO World Heritage Site. This park includes the impressive Durmitor Mountains, known for their deep gorges, crystal-clear lakes, and sharp peaks. The Tara River, which flows through the park, forms the deepest gorge in Europe, the Tara Canyon. Here, visitors can enjoy hiking, climbing, rafting, and a variety of other outdoor activities.

Another notable national park is the Biogradska Gora National Park, which is home to one of the last primeval forests in Europe. This park is famous for its ancient beech forest and Lake Biograd, which is fed by crystal clear waters. The park is a haven for nature lovers and birdwatchers, with plenty of hiking trails and opportunities to explore unspoiled nature.

The Prokletije Mountains, also known as the "Cursed Mountains", stretch along the border with Albania and Kosovo and are another important national park in Montenegro. This mountain range is characterized by spectacular peaks, deep gorges and wild rivers. The park is home to abundant wildlife, including brown bears, wolves, and lynxes, and is a popular destination for trekking and mountaineering.

Lake Skadar, the largest lake in the Balkans, is also an important nature reserve in Montenegro. This wetland is an important habitat for birds and fish and a popular destination for birdwatchers and nature lovers. The lake also offers boat trips and the opportunity to explore the historic islands and monasteries in the area.

Lovćen National Park is known for its majestic peak, Jezerski vrh, which is crowned by an impressive mausoleum dedicated to Montenegrin poet and national hero Petar II Petrović-Njegoš. This park offers spectacular views of the Bay of Kotor and is a popular destination for hiking and cultural experiences.

Montenegro also has nature reserves that protect a variety of habitats and animal species, including wetlands, forests, and coastal regions. These areas are important refuges for wildlife and offer visitors the opportunity to experience Montenegro's unspoiled nature.

The national parks and nature reserves in Montenegro are a treasure worth preserving and appreciating. Not only do they offer stunning natural scenery, but they also offer the opportunity to discover the country's unique wildlife and rich cultural history. Montenegro is a paradise for nature lovers and adventurers who want to experience the beauty and diversity of nature in its purest form.

The Adriatic coast of Montenegro

The Adriatic coast of Montenegro stretches over a length of about 293 kilometers along the eastern coast of the Adriatic Sea and is one of the most beautiful and unspoiled stretches of coastline in Europe. This coastal region is a true gem, characterized by majestic mountains, deep blue waters, and quaint towns.

One of the most famous cities on the Adriatic coast is Budva, which is often referred to as "Montenegro's pearl". Budva is famous for its historic old town, which is surrounded by a well-preserved city wall. Here you will find narrow streets, medieval churches, cozy cafes and restaurants. Budva's Old Town is a popular destination for tourists who want to experience the history and picturesque atmosphere.

Another highlight on the Adriatic coast is Kotor, a city known for its stunning location at the end of a fjord-like bay. The old town of Kotor is a UNESCO World Heritage Site and impresses with its well-preserved medieval architecture. The narrow streets, the cathedral of Kotor and the view from the city walls are impressive sights.

The Adriatic coast of Montenegro also offers numerous beaches, ranging from fine sand to gravel. Some of the most popular beaches are Jaz Beach, Mogren Beach, and Bečići Beach. These beaches are ideal for swimming, sunbathing and water sports such as windsurfing and diving.

The coast is lined with picturesque bays and islands, including the Bay of Kotor and the island of Sveti Stefan. The Bay of Kotor, also known as "Bocche di Cattaro", is a masterpiece of nature, surrounded by high mountains and separated from the Adriatic Sea by a narrow entrance. The island of Sveti Stefan was once a fishing village, which has now been converted into a luxury resort and is known worldwide.

The Adriatic coast of Montenegro is also a paradise for nature lovers, as it is surrounded by the mountains of the country. The view of the deep blue water against the backdrop of the imposing mountains is an impressive panorama that captivates visitors.

The coastal region offers a wide range of leisure activities, including hiking, water sports, boat trips and exploring the historic towns. Montenegro's Mediterranean cuisine, characterized by fresh seafood, olive oil, and local ingredients, is another highlight that visitors can enjoy.

The Adriatic coast of Montenegro is a place of outstanding natural beauty and cultural significance. It attracts tourists from all over the world who want to explore the unspoiled nature, rich history, and picturesque towns of this coastal region. This coast is a true jewel of the Mediterranean and offers unforgettable experiences for every visitor.

The beaches and bays of Montenegro

Montenegro, with its impressive Adriatic coast, is home to some of the most beautiful beaches and bays in Europe. The coastline stretches for about 293 kilometers and offers a variety of beaches ranging from fine sand to gravel. These picturesque stretches of coastline attract tourists from all over the world every year who want to enjoy the beauty and diversity of Montenegro's beaches and bays.

One of the most famous beaches on the Montenegrin coast is Jaz Beach. This expansive sandy beach is located near Budva and offers crystal clear waters and a relaxed atmosphere. Jaz Beach is also a popular venue for music festivals and concerts, attracting music lovers from all over the world.

Bečići Beach is another popular beach near Budva. Considered one of the best beaches in Europe, it offers fine sand, deep blue waters, and a variety of water sports. The promenade along the beach is lined with restaurants, bars and cafes serving local and international cuisine.

Mogren Beach is a smaller but picturesque beach in Budva surrounded by rocky cliffs. This beach is ideal for snorkeling and swimming and offers a quieter atmosphere than some of the larger beaches in the area.

The Bay of Kotor, also known as "Bocche di Cattaro", is home to some of the most beautiful bays and beaches in Montenegro. The bay stretches over 28 kilometers and offers numerous small bays and islands that invite you to explore. The villages of Perast and Herceg Novi are famous for their picturesque bays and offer great swimming opportunities.

The island of Sveti Stefan, a former fishing village, is now a luxury resort and has its own beach. The island is connected to the mainland by a headland and offers breathtaking views of the Adriatic Sea.

The beaches and bays of Montenegro offer not only the opportunity for sunbathing and swimming, but also numerous activities such as diving, water skiing, kayaking and jet skiing. The clear waters and picturesque scenery make these beaches a paradise for water sports enthusiasts.

The Mediterranean coast of Montenegro, characterized by rugged cliffs, picturesque bays and endless beaches, is a true jewel of the Mediterranean. The variety of beaches and bays offers something special for every visitor, making Montenegro a popular destination for beach lovers and nature lovers alike.

The Bay of Kotor and its history

The Bay of Kotor, also known as "Bocche di Cattaro", is one of the most impressive and fascinating landscapes in Montenegro and in the entire Mediterranean. This deeply cut bay stretches for 28 kilometers along the Adriatic coast and is framed by high mountain ranges that drop steeply into the crystal-clear water. The Bay of Kotor not only has stunning natural beauty, but also a rich history that makes it a UNESCO World Heritage Site.

The history of the Bay of Kotor dates back centuries, to ancient times. Even the Romans appreciated the strategic importance of this bay and founded important trading posts here. In the Middle Ages, the bay became a center of trade and culture, which led to the emergence of cities such as Kotor, Perast and Herceg Novi. These cities developed into thriving trading metropolises that were under different rulers, including the Venetians, the Byzantines and the Ottomans.

The town of Kotor, located at the southern end of the bay, is one of the outstanding historical gems in Montenegro. The well-preserved medieval old town of Kotor is surrounded by an imposing city wall and is home to numerous churches, palaces and museums. The Cathedral of Kotor, located in the Old Town, is a masterpiece of Romanesque-Gothic architecture and a highlight for history and art lovers.

Perast, a small town on the Bay of Kotor, was once an important trading port and is known for its Baroque architecture and the islands of Gospa od Škrpjela (Ons-Frauen-von-den-Felsen) and Sveti Đorđe (St. George). The island of Our Lady of Škrpjela is artificially created and houses a chapel decorated with precious paintings and silver offerings.

The Bay of Kotor has also played an important military role throughout history, as it was difficult to conquer due to its deep inlets and narrow passages. The Ottomans and Venetians fought centuries-long battles for control of the bay, resulting in a rich military history.

Today, the Bay of Kotor is a popular destination for tourists from all over the world. The quaint towns, dramatic scenery, and historic sites make it a unique place. The bay offers not only cultural and historical treasures, but also opportunities for outdoor activities such as hiking, boating and water sports.

The Bay of Kotor is not only a place of outstanding natural beauty and cultural significance, but also a living testimony to the eventful history of Montenegro and the region. It remains a fascinating destination for travelers who want to explore the past and the splendor of this unique bay.

Budva: history and sights

Budva, one of the oldest cities on the Montenegrin Adriatic coast, has a rich history and is now a significant tourist center. The city of Budva is located in the southwest of Montenegro and is surrounded by a picturesque coastal landscape. The history of Budva dates back over 2,500 years, and its historical sights tell of the different civilizations and cultures that have shaped this region.

The origins of Budva can be traced back to the time of the Illyrians, who inhabited the region before the Roman conquest. Under Roman rule, Budva flourished and became an important trading center. The Roman influences are still visible today in the remains of Roman villas, mosaics and city walls.

During the Byzantine era, Budva was an important religious center with numerous churches and monasteries. The city changed hands many times over the centuries, and the Ottomans, Venetians, and Austrians left their mark on Budva's architecture and culture.

One of the outstanding sights in Budva is the historic Old Town, which is surrounded by an impressive city wall. The Old Town of Budva is a maze of narrow streets, stone houses, medieval churches and squares. The Church of

St. John, a Romanesque church dating back to the 7th century, is one of the oldest buildings in the Old Town and an impressive example of religious architecture.

Another notable sight in Budva is the Citadel, which sits on a hill above the Old Town. The citadel was built during the Venetian rule in the 15th century and offers panoramic views of the coast and the surrounding sea.

Budva is also known for its beaches, including Jaz Beach, Slovenska Beach, and Mogren Beach. These beaches offer crystal clear waters and are ideal for sunbathing and swimming.

The city has become a popular tourist destination in recent decades and offers a wide range of entertainment options, including restaurants, bars, clubs, and festivals. The annual summer festivals in Budva attract artists and visitors from all over the world and offer a diverse cultural program.

Budva is not only a historical jewel, but also a lively place that combines tradition and modernity. The city is a magnet for travelers who want to explore Montenegro's rich history, impressive architecture, and stunning coastline.

The Old Town of Kotor and its Significance

The old town of Kotor, located in the heart of the Bay of Kotor, is one of the best-preserved medieval towns in the entire Mediterranean. This historic city has a history of over 2,000 years and is not only a national treasure of Montenegro, but also a UNESCO World Heritage Site. The importance of the old town of Kotor extends far beyond the country's borders, attracting thousands of visitors year after year.

The origins of the city date back to Roman times, when it was founded under the name of "Acruvium". Later, the city was settled by the Byzantines and Slavs before it came under Venetian rule in the 12th century. This long and diverse history has shaped the city's architecture and cultural heritage.

The old town of Kotor is surrounded by an imposing city wall that stretches for 4.5 kilometers and is enthroned on a steep hill. Built in the 9th century and expanded and strengthened over the centuries, this wall is an impressive example of medieval fortification. The city wall is a symbol of the city's defensive capability and today offers spectacular views of the bay and the surrounding countryside.

The heart of the Old Town is the Main Square, also known as "Trg od Oružja" or Weapons Square. Here you will find the Cathedral of Kotor, a masterpiece of Romanesque architecture dating back to the 12th century. The cathedral houses the famous silver altarpiece by Giovanni Bellini and is a spiritual and cultural hub of the city.

The narrow streets and squares of the old town are lined with restored medieval buildings, including palaces, monasteries, churches and museums. The palaces of former noble families such as the Grgurina and the Pima bear witness to the historical importance of the city as a commercial and cultural center.

The old town of Kotor not only attracts history and culture lovers, but also offers a lively atmosphere with numerous cafes, restaurants, boutiques and art galleries. The alleys are lined with traditional local shops selling handmade souvenirs, jewellery and local products.

The old town of Kotor is not only a place of history and culture, but also a place of a vibrant community that is proud of its heritage. The annual festivals and events, such as the Kotor Festival and the Kotor Carnival, are highlights in the city's cultural calendar and attract visitors from all over the world.

The old town of Kotor and its significance extend far beyond the city limits, making it a treasure appreciated by UNESCO and the world public. It is a reflection of Montenegro's rich history and a place that deserves to be admired and preserved.

Cetinje: The historic capital of Montenegro

Cetinje, also known as "Cetinje Monastery" or "The City of Museums", is a city of great historical importance and was the capital of Montenegro for centuries. It is located in the central part of the country, in the middle of a picturesque mountain landscape and close to the Bay of Kotor. The history and culture of Cetinje reflect Montenegro's turbulent past.

The foundation of Cetinje dates back to the 15th century, when the monastery of the same name was built here. The Cetinje Monastery served as a religious and cultural center and quickly became an important place for the preservation of Montenegrin traditions and history. In the 19th century, Cetinje was declared the capital of Montenegro and remained so until the creation of the Kingdom of Yugoslavia in 1929.

The architecture of Cetinje is characterized by historical buildings, churches and palaces. One of the most important buildings in the city is the Royal Palace, which now houses a museum. The National Museum of Montenegro and the Museum of History and Art are other cultural institutions that vividly present the history and culture of the country.

The Cetinje Monastery, founded in the 15th century, is an important religious and cultural center. It houses valuable religious relics and historical documents that reflect the history of Montenegro.

Cetinje was not only the political and cultural center of Montenegro, but also a place of resistance against Ottoman rule. The city played an important role in the Montenegrin struggle for independence and became a symbol of the Montenegrin people's desire for freedom.

Today, Cetinje is a quiet and picturesque place that testifies to its historical importance. The city is surrounded by impressive nature and offers opportunities for hiking and exploring the surrounding mountains. Cetinje's museums and historical sites attract visitors who want to learn about Montenegro's rich history and culture.

Cetinje, the historic capital of Montenegro, remains a place of remembrance and a living testimony to the identity and pride of the Montenegrin people. The city has retained its historical significance and is now a place of cultural heritage and education, valued by the world community.

Podgorica: Moderne Metropole im Landesinneren

Podgorica, the capital of Montenegro, is a modern inland metropolis that contrasts with the historical splendor of the country's coastal cities. The city is located in the central part of Montenegro and has developed into an important political, economic and cultural center over the decades. The history of Podgorica is marked by various dominations and changes that have made the city what it is today.

The origins of Podgorica date back to Roman times, when the city was known as "Doclea". In the following centuries, the city changed its name and rule several times, including the Ottoman rule, under which it bore the name "Üsküp". It was not until the 20th century that the city was given the name Podgorica and became the capital of independent Montenegro.

During World War II, Podgorica was severely destroyed, but in the post-war period, the city was rebuilt and modernized. Today, Podgorica is the economic center of Montenegro, which is home to a variety of industries and services. The city is home to numerous international companies, embassies and institutions.

Podgorica is characterized by modern architecture, which differs from the historical buildings of coastal towns. The city centre is characterised by office buildings, shopping centres and residential complexes. The city center is crisscrossed by wide boulevards and offers a variety of restaurants, cafes and shops.

The city has cultural institutions such as the Montenegrin National Theatre and the Municipal Cultural Centre, which offer a wide range of cultural events and performances. The Archaeological Museum of Montenegro and the Museum of Contemporary Art are also important cultural institutions in the city.

Although Podgorica is rather modern, there are also historical sights, including the old Ottoman bridge "Stari Most" and the remains of the fortress "Gorica". The Moraca River, which flows through the town, offers opportunities for outdoor activities such as hiking and rafting.

Podgorica is also a transport hub, as Podgorica International Airport is located close to the city and provides easy access to the Montenegrin road network.

Overall, Podgorica is a modern inland metropolis that is different from the coastal cities of Montenegro, but still plays an important role in the political, economic and cultural life of the country. The city reflects the dynamism and diversity of Montenegro and is an important part of the country's identity.

Bar: Historic harbour and cultural city

Bar, a town on the Montenegrin Adriatic coast, is a place of great historical importance and cultural richness. The history of Bar dates back to ancient times, and the city has been home to different civilizations and cultures over the centuries, highlighting its cultural diversity and historical significance.

The origins of Bar can be traced back to Roman times, when the town was known as "Antivari". During this time, Bar was an important port and a trading center on the Adriatic coast. Later, the city was controlled by the Byzantines, Venetians, and Ottomans, resulting in a rich cultural heritage.

A significant historical feature of Bar is the old town of Stari Bar, which is located a little inland from the present-day town. Stari Bar was once an important trading post and a major crossroads on the trade route between Venice and the East. The old town is surrounded by an imposing city wall and is home to historic buildings, churches and mosques that reflect the city's eventful history.

Bar was also a place of cultural exchange between the West and the East. This is evident in the city's architecture, which has both Venetian and Ottoman influences. The Ottomans left behind numerous historic buildings and a diverse cultural heritage.

The city is also known for its rich religious diversity. Bar is home to Christian churches, including the impressive St. Catherine's Church, but also mosques such as the Ottoman Mosque, which underline the city's multi-religious history.

The modern part of Bar is an important port and economic center of Montenegro. The Port of Bar is the largest port in Montenegro and plays an important role in the country's trade and tourism. The town is also a popular tourist destination, especially for those who want to explore the historic old town of Stari Bar and enjoy the natural beauty of the surrounding area.

Overall, Bar is a city with a fascinating history that has been shaped by different cultures and civilizations. The historic old town, modern harbor and diverse culture make Bar an important place in Montenegro that reflects the country's history and identity.

Herceg Novi: Pearl of the Bay of Kotor

Herceg Novi, a charming town on the Adriatic coast in Montenegro, is often referred to as the "Pearl of the Bay of Kotor". Located at the entrance to the impressive Bay of Kotor, the city has a rich history, stunning scenery and a variety of cultural treasures.

The origins of Herceg Novi date back to the Byzantine period, when the city was founded under the name "Sveti Stefan". Over the centuries, the city changed hands several times and was shaped by various civilizations, including the Byzantines, Venetians, Ottomans, and Montenegrins. This diverse history has made Herceg Novi a place with a unique cultural mix.

One of the most famous sights of Herceg Novi is the fortress "Fortica" or "Kanli Kula", which towers high above the city. This fortress was built by the Ottomans in the 16th century and offers spectacular panoramic views of the Bay of Kotor and the surrounding area.

The old town of Herceg Novi is a picturesque place with narrow streets, cobbled squares and historic buildings. St. Michael's Church and St. Jeremiah's Church are just a few of the religious sites that adorn the Old Town. The city is also known for its numerous stairs and steps that connect the different levels of the city.

Herceg Novi has a rich cultural scene and is known for its summer festivals, including the Herceg Novi Film Festival and the Dani Mimoze Music Festival. These events attract artists and visitors from all over the world and enrich the cultural life of the city.

The city is surrounded by lush Mediterranean vegetation and offers numerous opportunities for outdoor activities such as hiking, water sports and boat trips. The beaches of Herceg Novi are popular destinations for sun worshippers and water sports enthusiasts.

Herceg Novi also has a rich culinary scene, offering local specialties such as fresh fish, seafood, and Mediterranean dishes. The cafes and restaurants in the town invite visitors to enjoy the delicious Montenegrin cuisine.

Overall, Herceg Novi is a charming town that combines history, culture, and nature. The "Pearl of the Bay of Kotor" offers a unique atmosphere and is a popular destination for tourists who want to experience the beauty and charm of Montenegro's Adriatic coast.

Ulcinj: The southernmost city of Montenegro

Ulcinj, the southernmost city in Montenegro, is located on the Adriatic coast and is a city of great historical importance and natural beauty. The history of Ulcinj goes back a long way and reflects the cultural diversity and eventful history of the region.

The origins of Ulcinj can be traced back to ancient times, when the town was an important trading town and port under the name "Olcinium". Over the centuries, Ulcinj has been controlled by various civilizations, including the Romans, Byzantines, Venetians, and Ottomans. This diverse history has shaped the architecture and culture of the city.

One of the most famous landmarks of Ulcinj is the Ulcinj Fortress, also known as the Fortress of Rosafa. This fortress dates back to the Ottoman era and offers impressive views of the city and the surrounding countryside.

The Old Town of Ulcinj is a picturesque place with narrow streets, historic buildings and a lively market square. The Great Mosque of Ulcinj, the Small Mosque and the Church of St. Nicholas are just some of the religious sites that reflect the diversity of cultures in the city.

Ulcinj is also known for its impressive beaches, including the 13-kilometer Velika Plaza, one of the longest sandy beaches on the Adriatic coast. The beaches of Ulcinj attract bathers and water sports enthusiasts from all over the world.

The city has a rich culinary tradition, characterized by its proximity to the sea and the various cultural influences. Fish and seafood are popular specialties in the restaurants of Ulcinj.

Ulcinj is also an important place for bird migration, as the city is on the route of many migratory birds. Lake Ada near Ulcinj is an important nature reserve and a paradise for birdwatchers.

Overall, Ulcinj is a city that combines history, culture and nature. Montenegro's southernmost city attracts visitors with its beauty, beaches, and rich history. Ulcinj is a place that uniquely reflects the diversity and charm of Montenegro.

The Eastern Cape of Montenegro

The Eastern Cape of Montenegro is a stunning region that stretches along the Adriatic coast and is characterized by natural beauty as well as historical richness. This coastal region of Montenegro is known not only for its picturesque landscapes, but also for its cultural diversity and historical significance.

The coast of the Eastern Cape of Montenegro stretches from the southern town of Ulcinj to the town of Bar. This region is characterized by its spectacular beaches, including the famous Velika Plaza, one of the longest sandy beaches on the Adriatic coast. The coast offers numerous bays, hidden coves and crystal clear waters, making it a paradise for sun worshippers and water sports enthusiasts.

One of the most notable sights of the Eastern Cape is the city of Ulcinj, the southernmost city in Montenegro. Ulcinj has a rich history that has been shaped by various civilizations, including the Romans, Byzantines, Venetians, and Ottomans. The Old Town of Ulcinj is a historical treasure with narrow streets, historic buildings and religious sites that reflect the cultural diversity of the city.

In addition to Ulcinj, the Eastern Cape of Montenegro also offers the town of Bar, which is an important port and economic center of the country. The Old Town of Bar, also known as Stari Bar, is another historical gem that was shaped by the Ottomans. The Kanli Kula Fortress, high above the city, offers a breathtaking view of the surrounding area.

The coast of the Eastern Cape of Montenegro is also characterized by numerous natural beauties. The hinterland of the region is characterized by mountains and lush Mediterranean vegetation. Lake Ada near Ulcinj is an important nature reserve and a paradise for birdwatchers.

In terms of cuisine, the coast of the Eastern Cape of Montenegro offers an abundance of seafood, fish dishes and Mediterranean delicacies. The restaurants in the region serve fresh local products and offer guests an authentic culinary experience.

The Eastern Cape of Montenegro is a region of incredible diversity that combines history, culture, nature and recreation. The coastal landscape, historic towns, and natural beauties make this region a sought-after destination for visitors who want to discover the treasures of Montenegro.

The historical significance of Eastern Montenegro

Eastern Montenegro, also known as the eastern part of Montenegro, is a region of great historical importance that stands out for its rich history and cultural diversity. This region, which stretches east of the capital Podgorica, has witnessed various civilizations and influences over the centuries that have shaped its historical significance.

The history of Eastern Montenegro dates back to ancient times, when this region was inhabited by various Illyrian tribes. Over time, the area was conquered by the Romans and became part of the Roman Empire. This period left behind numerous archaeological sites that indicate the Roman presence in the region.

During the Middle Ages, Eastern Montenegro played an important role in the Byzantine Empire and was a center of Orthodox Christianity. Monasteries such as the Moraca Monastery and the Ostrog Monastery are testimonies to this religious tradition and still attract believers and pilgrims today.

Later, the region was conquered by various powers, including the Venetians, Ottomans, and Austrians. This eventful history is reflected in the architecture and culture of Eastern Montenegro. The city of Bar, one of the largest cities in the region, became an important trading center during the Ottoman rule and a crossroads on the trade route between Venice and the East.

During the First World War, Eastern Montenegro played a crucial role in the events of the Balkans and contributed to the emergence of modern Montenegro. The city of Podgorica, which is now the capital of the country, was an important strategic place during the war.

The historical importance of eastern Montenegro is also evident in the numerous fortresses, monasteries and historical buildings that adorn the region. These sights are not only witnesses of the past, but also important cultural and tourist attractions.

Overall, the historical significance of eastern Montenegro is a reflection of the eventful history of the Balkans and the cultural diversity that has shaped the region. These historical treasures are now an important part of Montenegro's heritage and invite visitors to discover the history and culture of this fascinating region.

The Orthodox monasteries of Montenegro

Montenegro is known for its impressive landscape, historic cities and rich cultural traditions. One of the most distinctive and fascinating aspects of Montenegrin culture is the Orthodox monasteries scattered throughout the region, which play an important role in the country's religious and cultural life.

The Moraca Monastery is one of the most important Orthodox monasteries in Montenegro. It was founded in the 13th century and is located near Kolasin in a picturesque mountainous region. The architecture of the Moraca Monastery is impressive, and its frescoes are a masterpiece of medieval art. The monastery also houses an important collection of religious relics and treasures.

Ostrog Monastery is another famous Orthodox monastery in Montenegro and an important pilgrimage site. It was founded in the 17th century and is located in the mountains above the town of Niksic. The monastery is built into the rock and impresses with its white facades and its churches decorated with icons. Thousands of believers visit the Ostrog Monastery every year to pray and invoke the miraculous healing power of St. Vasilije of Ostrog.

The Cetinje Monastery is a historical and cultural gem in Montenegro. It was founded in the 15th century and for a long time served as the residence of the Montenegrin Metropolitan. The monastery houses an impressive collection of icons, relics and liturgical objects. The church of the monastery is a magnificent example of Montenegrin Orthodox architecture.

The Savina Monastery is located near the town of Herceg Novi and is one of the oldest monasteries in Montenegro. It was founded in the 13th century and is characterized by its quiet location on the shore of the Bay of Kotor. The frescoes in the monastery's church are well preserved and offer insights into the religious art of the Middle Ages.

These Orthodox monasteries are just a selection of the many monasteries that can be found in Montenegro. They are not only religious sites, but also important cultural and historical places that shape Montenegro's heritage and identity. Visitors have the opportunity to experience the spiritual atmosphere of these monasteries and discover the rich history and art of Montenegro.

Montenegro's fortifications and castles

Montenegro is rich in historic fortifications and castles that reflect the country's eventful history. These impressive structures tell stories of conquests, defenses, and the strategic importance of Montenegro over the centuries.

One of the most famous fortresses in Montenegro is the Kotor Fortress. Perched high above the UNESCO World Heritage city of Kotor, this imposing castle offers not only breathtaking views of the Bay of Kotor, but also glimpses of medieval defensive architecture. The fortress of Kotor was built in the 9th century and expanded and strengthened over time by various rulers.

The Budva Fortress is another important historical structure. It is located in the old town of Budva and offers a panoramic view of the Adriatic Sea. The fortress was built in the 15th century and played an important role in the defense of the city against the Ottomans and Venetians.

In the town of Herceg Novi, the Forte Mare fortress rises majestically above the Bay of Kotor. This fortress was built by the Bosnians in the 14th century and later conquered by the Ottomans. Today, it is a symbol of the city and a popular vantage point for visitors.

The fortress of Bar, also known as Stari Bar or the old town of Bar, is another impressive historical structure. This fortress was built during the Ottoman rule and served as an important trading post. The well-preserved complex includes towers, gates, mosques and a rich history.

The Petrovac Fortress is a picturesque castle near the coastal town of Petrovac. It was built by the Venetians in the 16th century and is surrounded by Mediterranean vegetation. The views from this fortress of the sea and coastline are breathtaking.

These examples are just a selection of the many fortresses and castles in Montenegro. They bear witness to the diversity of cultures and influences that have shaped the country's history and invite visitors to immerse themselves in Montenegro's past and explore its imposing structures.

The UNESCO World Heritage Sites in Montenegro

Montenegro is home to a remarkable number of UNESCO World Heritage Sites that reflect the country's cultural and natural diversity. These sites have been included in the prestigious UNESCO World Heritage List due to their exceptional importance to humanity and nature and are an important part of Montenegro's national heritage.

The old town of Kotor, which stretches along the shores of the Bay of Kotor, is one of the most outstanding World Heritage sites in Montenegro. This well-preserved medieval town is surrounded by imposing city walls and is home to an impressive collection of historic buildings, churches, palaces and narrow streets. The Old Town of Kotor was included in the UNESCO World Heritage List due to its architectural and historical significance and today attracts visitors from all over the world.

The Bay of Kotor itself is also recognized as a UNESCO World Heritage Site. This spectacular bay is surrounded by high mountains and offers a unique scenic beauty. The Bay of Kotor is also an important habitat for various animal species and a historically important trading place.

The Ostrog Monastery, located high in the mountains of eastern Montenegro, is another World Heritage Site that has religious and cultural significance. The monastery was built into the rock and attracts thousands of pilgrims and believers every year who visit the holy site to pray and seek healing.

Durmitor National Park, with its majestic mountain massif and deep gorges, is a natural World Heritage Site that highlights the beauty of the Montenegrin landscape. The park is home to a variety of animal and plant species and offers outdoor activities such as hiking and rafting.

Biogradska Gora National Park, another natural heritage site in Montenegro, is known for its ancient forest and Lake Biograd. This park is one of the last relics of Europe's pristine forests and offers a glimpse of Montenegro's unspoiled nature.

Montenegro is proud of its UNESCO World Heritage Sites, which highlight not only the beauty of the country, but also its cultural and natural diversity. These sites are a precious heritage and invite visitors to explore Montenegro's rich history and stunning nature.

Top Montenegro's Water Sports Facilities

Montenegro, with its picturesque Adriatic coast and numerous lakes and rivers, offers a wealth of water sports for adventurers and nature lovers alike. The variety of waters and spectacular scenery make Montenegro a prime destination for water sports activities.

The Adriatic coast of Montenegro stretches for 293 kilometers along the eastern coast of the Adriatic Sea and offers countless opportunities for sailing and surfing. Conditions in the Bay of Kotor are particularly favorable for sailors, as the sheltered waters are great for boating. The coast also offers ideal conditions for windsurfers, kitesurfers and stand-up paddle boarding enthusiasts.

Lake Skadar, the largest lake in the Balkans, is a paradise for water sports enthusiasts. Here visitors can go canoeing, kayaking, rowing and fishing. The lake is home to a rich variety of waterfowl and also offers the opportunity to take boat trips to the numerous islands of the lake.

The Tara Gorge, a UNESCO World Heritage Site, is a popular destination for whitewater rafting adventures. One of the cleanest rivers in Europe, the Tara River flows through the spectacular gorge, offering thrilling rapids and breathtaking views of the surrounding landscape.

Montenegro is also a popular diving destination, as the clear waters of the Adriatic Sea and the numerous underwater caves and reefs are home to impressive marine life. Divers can explore various marine life and wrecks here.

The numerous lakes and rivers inland offer opportunities for fishing, canoeing and swimming. Lake Biograd, one of the largest lakes in Montenegro, is particularly popular for water sports activities.

In conclusion, Montenegro offers a wide range of water sports for those who want to enjoy the beauty of the waters and the nature of the country. Whether you want to sail, surf, dive, rafting, fish or just swim, Montenegro has a lot to offer for water sports enthusiasts.

Hiking and outdoor activities in Montenegro

Montenegro is a true paradise for nature and outdoor enthusiasts who want to explore the unspoiled beauty of the Montenegrin countryside. The country's diverse topography offers a wide range of hiking and outdoor activities that appeal to adventure seekers and nature lovers alike.

The Montenegrin Alps, including Durmitor and Prokletije National Park, are popular destinations for hikers. Here you will find well-marked hiking trails that lead through dense forests, alpine meadows and majestic peaks. Durmitor National Park offers the highest peak in the country, Bobotov Kuk, which offers breathtaking views of the surrounding mountain landscape. In the Prokletije Mountains you can discover rare animal species and unique flora.

The Tara Canyon, the deepest canyon in Europe, is another paradise for outdoor activities. Here you can experience white water rafting, kayaking and canyoning. The Tara River offers exciting rapids and crystal clear waters that are perfect for rafting.

Montenegro's lakes are ideal places for canoeing, kayaking and swimming. Lake Skadar and Lake Biograd are particularly popular destinations for water activities. Lake Biograd is also home to the Biograd National Park, which offers numerous hiking trails and nature trails.

For mountaineers and climbers, Montenegro offers a variety of climbing routes and via ferratas. The Komovi massif and Rumija mountain are well-known climbing areas that offer challenges for climbing enthusiasts.

In winter, the Montenegrin mountains turn into a paradise for skiers and snowboarders. The ski resorts in Kolasin and Zabljak offer slopes for all levels and a picturesque winter landscape.

In addition to the mountains and waters, Montenegro also offers opportunities for mountain biking, paragliding, horseback riding and bird watching. The variety of outdoor activities in Montenegro makes the country a year-round destination for adventure seekers.

Montenegro's unspoiled nature, abundant wildlife, and breathtaking scenery invite you to experience the country's beauty through hiking and outdoor activities. Whether you want to climb the peaks of the Alps, explore the gorges, or simply enjoy the tranquility of nature, Montenegro offers something special for every outdoor enthusiast.

Montenegro's traditional craftsmanship

Traditional craftsmanship in Montenegro reflects the country's rich cultural history and rural ways of life. Over the centuries, Montenegrin artisans have developed various skills and techniques to create handicrafts of the highest quality, often passed down from generation to generation.

One of the most well-known forms of craftsmanship in Montenegro is the production of carpets and textiles. Carpet making is a lengthy process that involves collecting wool from local sheep and spinning it by hand. The carpets are then woven by hand and decorated with traditional patterns and motifs. These carpets are not only works of art, but also practical everyday objects.

The production of ceramics is another important form of craftsmanship in Montenegro. Potters in different regions of the country produce pottery such as pots, vases and tableware. These ceramics are often decorated with regional patterns and ornaments and reflect the diversity of Montenegrin culture.

Wood carving is an old tradition in Montenegro, where artistic woodwork is made. Woodcarvers use local woods to create sculptures, pieces of furniture, and religious artwork. These craftsmen are known for their precise work and attention to detail.

Jewelry making is also an important form of craftsmanship in Montenegro. Silversmiths create elaborate pieces of jewellery that often represent traditional motifs and symbols of the country. These pieces of jewelry are popular souvenirs for tourists and are also worn on festive occasions.

Montenegro's traditional craftsmanship is an important part of the country's cultural heritage and continues to be nurtured and appreciated. The craftsmen continue their craft with passion and pride, and the works of art they create are a testament to Montenegro's rich history and culture. Visitors to the country have the opportunity to experience these traditional crafts first-hand and take a piece of Montenegrin history home with them.

The Montenegrins and their hospitality

The hospitality of Montenegrins is an integral part of their culture and identity. In Montenegro, guests are often seen as a "gift from God", and the locals always strive to give their guests a warm welcome and hospitality. Montenegrins are known for their sincere kindness and generosity towards visitors from all over the world.

One of the most notable qualities of Montenegrin hospitality is the willingness to invite guests into their homes and share with them. It is not uncommon for locals to invite strangers to dinner or offer them a cup of Turkish coffee. These gestures of hospitality are deeply rooted in the culture and show the open nature of Montenegrins.

In Montenegro, hospitality is also emphasized by the tradition of the "Kumstvo" or the "Kumovi". This is a close friendship relationship that is often formed between families. The Kumovi are responsible for each other and share common joys and sorrows. This connection often extends to hospitality to visitors and ensures that guests are always in good hands in Montenegro.

Montenegrin cuisine also plays an important role in the country's hospitality. Locals take pride in their traditional dishes and are always willing to share them with guests. Whether it's "cevapi" (grilled sausage), "prsuta" (air-dried ham) or "sarma" (cabbage rolls), Montenegrin cuisine offers a wealth of culinary experiences.

Montenegrin hospitality is also evident in the numerous festivals and celebrations in the country. Visitors are welcome to take part in the traditional festivals that focus on music, dancing and delicious food. These events are a great opportunity to experience local culture first-hand and connect with locals.

In conclusion, the hospitality of Montenegrins is a central part of their identity. Visitors to Montenegro are warmly welcomed and often feel part of the community. Montenegrins are proud of their culture and like to share it with others. This makes Montenegro a welcoming and warm-hearted destination for people from all over the world.

Travel and accommodation in Montenegro

Montenegro has become an increasingly popular destination in recent years, offering a variety of options for travelers who want to explore the country. From stunning natural landscapes to historic towns and quaint coastal towns, Montenegro has something for everyone.

Getting to Montenegro is relatively easy, as the country has two international airports: Podgorica Airport and Tivat Airport. Both airports are well connected to various European cities, making it easy to get there. Alternatively, you can also come into the country by car via the well-developed roads and motorways.

When choosing accommodation, travelers in Montenegro have a wide range at their disposal. From luxurious 5-star hotels to cozy guesthouses and apartments, there are accommodations to suit all tastes and budgets. In the coastal towns such as Budva, Kotor and Herceg Novi, you will find a variety of hotels overlooking the Adriatic Sea. In the mountains, there are rustic mountain huts and country inns that are perfect for hikers and nature lovers. Getting around Montenegro is also uncomplicated. The country has a well-developed road network that makes traveling by car or bus easy. There are also regular ferry services to the islands and along the coast. The Montenegrins are friendly and helpful, so it is easy to find your way around even as a foreign tourist. Montenegro offers a wealth of activities for travelers. The Adriatic coast is a paradise for sun worshippers and water sports enthusiasts, with numerous beaches, water sports and boat trips. The country's mountains offer great opportunities for hiking, climbing, and mountain biking. Historic cities such as Kotor and Cetinje are rich in culture and history and invite you to explore.

The local cuisine in Montenegro is diverse and delicious. Be sure to try the traditional dishes such as "cevapi" (grilled sausage), "burek" (stuffed pasta) and "riblja corba" (fish soup). It goes well with a glass of local wine or a sip of the famous rakija, a fruit brandy.

Montenegro also has numerous events and festivals that take place throughout the year. From music festivals to religious celebrations, there is always something to experience and discover.

In conclusion, Montenegro is a diverse and fascinating destination. With its breathtaking nature, rich history and warm hospitality, the country offers unforgettable experiences for travelers from all over the world.

Transportation and Transportation in Montenegro

Getting around Montenegro is varied and straightforward, and there are various modes of transport to choose from to explore the country. From roads and highways to ferries and public transport, Montenegro offers good opportunities to move around the country.

Road network: Montenegro has a well-developed road network that connects the different regions of the country. The main connecting roads are usually in good condition and allow for a comfortable ride. The coastal road that runs along the Adriatic coast is particularly picturesque and offers spectacular views of the sea and mountains. There are also highways that connect the cities and reduce travel times.

Car rental: A popular way to explore Montenegro is to rent a car. In the larger cities and airports, there are car rental companies that offer a wide range of vehicles. This allows travelers to be flexible and explore remote places that are difficult to reach by public transport.

Buses: The bus network in Montenegro is well developed and connects most cities and regions in the country. Buses are a cost-effective way to get around and provide regular services between major cities. The buses are often modern and comfortable, and the schedules are usually reliable.

Trains: Montenegro also has a railway system that connects some cities. The trains are a leisurely way to explore the country, especially if you want to enjoy the picturesque scenery. However, the train services are not as frequent as the buses, so it is advisable to check the schedules in advance.

Ferries: Due to its coastal location, Montenegro also offers ferry services to the surrounding islands and along the Adriatic coast. This is a great way to explore different places and experience the beauty of the coast. The ferries are usually well organized and offer convenient travel options.

Taxi: Taxis are readily available in most cities in Montenegro and are a convenient way to get around the city. Prices vary depending on the city and distance, but they are generally affordable.

Cycling and hiking: Montenegro also offers great opportunities for cycling and hiking, especially in the mountains. There are many marked hiking trails and bike paths that lead the adventurous into the unspoiled nature of the country.

To sum up, Montenegro offers a variety of means of transport and ways to get around. Travelers can choose the best option to explore the country and discover the diverse sights and landscapes of Montenegro, depending on their preferences and needs.

Practical information for travellers

Before you start your trip to Montenegro, there is some practical information that can help you plan and during your stay. Here are some key facts and tips to keep in mind:

1. Travel documents: As an EU citizen, you only need a valid passport or identity card to enter Montenegro. Make sure your documents are valid for the entire duration of your stay.
2. Currency: The official currency in Montenegro is the Euro (EUR). ATMs are widely available in most cities and tourist areas, and credit cards are accepted in most hotels, restaurants, and shops.
3. Language: The official language in Montenegro is Montenegrin, but many people also speak English, especially in tourist areas. German and Italian are also often understood.
4. Time zone: Montenegro is located in the Central European Time Zone (CET), which is one hour ahead of Coordinated Universal Time (UTC+1). During daylight saving time (from the end of March to the end

of October), the clock is put forward by one hour to UTC+2.
5. Electricity: The electrical voltage in Montenegro is 230 volts at a frequency of 50 Hz. The sockets are Type C and F, so an adapter may be required.
6. Health and safety: Montenegro is a safe destination, but it is always advisable to check the current travel advice from your home country. There are no specific vaccination requirements for entering Montenegro, but it is recommended that you keep your vaccination status up to date.
7. Emergency numbers: The emergency number for the police in Montenegro is 122, for the fire brigade 123 and for medical emergencies 124. The general European emergency number 112 is also valid.
8. Transportation: As mentioned earlier, Montenegro offers various transportation options, including buses, trains, ferries, taxis, and rental cars. Prices vary depending on the mode of transport and route, but most are affordable.
9. Where to stay: Montenegro offers a wide range of accommodation, from luxury hotels to apartments to hostels

and guesthouses. It is advisable to book in advance, especially during the high season.
10. Things to see and do: Montenegro has a rich selection of things to see and do, including historic cities, national parks, beaches, water sports, hiking and more. Plan your itinerary in advance to get the most out of your stay.

This practical information should be useful to you in your travel preparation and during your stay in Montenegro. Remember to do your research in advance and plan your trip carefully to enjoy an unforgettable experience in this beautiful country.

Safety and health in Montenegro

The safety and health of travelers is of paramount importance when visiting Montenegro. This chapter covers important information about safety and health during your stay in Montenegro.

1. Safety:
    - Montenegro is considered a safe country to travel to, and crime against tourists is relatively rare. Nevertheless, you should take the usual precautions to protect your valuables and not be inattentive, especially in busy tourist areas.
2. Bless you:
    - Medical care in Montenegro is generally good, especially in larger cities such as Podgorica and Kotor. There are hospitals, clinics, and pharmacies that offer a wide range of medical services.
    - No special vaccinations are required to enter Montenegro. However, it is recommended that you keep your routine vaccinations up to date.

- Drinking water from the tap is usually safe, but in remote areas and mountainous regions, it may be better to resort to bottled water to avoid stomach problems.
- Sun protection is important because Montenegro is a sunny country. Use sunscreen, wear protective clothing, and avoid excessive sun exposure to prevent sunburn.
- Be sure to review your insurance policy to ensure that you are adequately covered in the event of a medical emergency.

3. Natural hazards:
   - Montenegro is vulnerable to natural hazards such as earthquakes and forest fires. Although such events are rare, it is advisable to learn about guidelines for conduct in the event of an emergency.

4. Traffic:
   - The traffic rules in Montenegro are similar to those in other European countries. Wearing seat belts and helmets is mandatory, and the alcohol limit for drinking

and driving is 0.03%. Drive carefully on the often winding roads and stick to speed limits.
5. Emergency numbers:
    o The emergency number for the police in Montenegro is 122, for medical emergencies 124 and for the fire brigade 123. The general European emergency number 112 is also valid.

It is important to follow the safety and health guidelines and to travel responsibly. Montenegro offers a fascinating environment, but like anywhere else in the world, you should take care of your safety and health to enjoy your trip to the fullest. Before traveling, find out about the current conditions and follow local recommendations to make your experience in this beautiful country safe and healthy.

Montenegro: Looking to the future

If we look into the future of Montenegro, we see a country that is constantly developing and strengthening its position in Europe and the world. Montenegro has made significant progress in recent years and faces a multitude of challenges and opportunities.

1. EU-Integration:
    - Montenegro is seeking membership in the European Union and has already achieved the status of an official EU accession candidate. Integration into the EU will further stabilise the country politically and economically.
2. Economic development:
    - The Montenegrin economy has developed positively in recent years, especially in the tourism sector, which has become an important economic engine. Investment in infrastructure and tourism is expected to continue to grow.
3. Natural treasures and environmental protection:

- Montenegro has an impressive natural diversity that needs to be protected. The establishment of national parks and nature reserves will promote the sustainable use of natural resources.
4. Cultural heritage:
    - The rich cultural history of Montenegro continues to be cherished and appreciated. The preservation of historic cities, Orthodox monasteries and traditional crafts will preserve the cultural identity of the country.
5. Tourism and hospitality:
    - Montenegro has the potential to become one of the most popular tourist destinations in Europe. The picturesque Adriatic coast, the Bay of Kotor and the breathtaking nature attract tourists from all over the world.
6. Challenges:
    - Montenegro faces challenges such as the fight against corruption, the modernisation of education systems and the safeguarding of water

resources. Overcoming these challenges will be crucial.
7. Geopolitical situation:
    o Montenegro's geopolitical location in the Balkans makes it an important player in the region. The country is striving for stability and cooperation with its neighbours.

Montenegro undoubtedly has a promising future ahead of it, in which it can consolidate its place in Europe and the world. Efforts to integrate into the EU, promote tourism and preserve its natural and cultural treasures will play a key role in shaping this future. It remains to be seen how the country will develop in the coming years, but the outlook is promising.

Closing remarks

In this book, we took a journey through Montenegro, a fascinating country rich in history, culture, and natural beauty. We explored the different aspects of this country, from its geographical diversity to its turbulent history to its hospitable people and promising future prospects.

Montenegro, which is often referred to as the "Pearl of the Adriatic", has experienced significant development in recent years. Integration into the European Union is imminent and will continue to support the country on its path to stability and economic prosperity.

The stunning Adriatic coast with its picturesque beaches and bays, the impressive Bay of Kotor and the historic cities such as Kotor, Budva, Cetinje and Herceg Novi attract tourists from all over the world. Montenegro's rich cultural history is reflected in its Orthodox monasteries, traditional crafts and culinary delights.

The country's natural beauties, including national parks and nature reserves, are priceless and must be protected and preserved. Montenegro's commitment to environmental protection and sustainability is an important step in this direction.

The Montenegrin population is known for its hospitality and openness to visitors. This feature makes traveling in Montenegro a unique and enriching experience.

Montenegro undoubtedly has a promising future ahead of it. It remains to be seen how the country will develop in the coming years, but the course has been set. With its rich resources and strategic location in the Balkans, Montenegro will continue to play an important role in the region.

We hope that this book has provided you with a comprehensive and informative introduction to Montenegro and inspires you to explore this beautiful country on your own. May Montenegro continue to flourish and preserve its uniqueness.

Printed in Great Britain
by Amazon